An Outline of Theosophy

By C. W. Leadbeater

Copyright © 2019 Lamp of Trismegistus. All rights reserved. No part of this publication may be reproduced or transmitted in any form or by any means, electronic or mechanical, including photocopying, recording, or by any information storage and retrieval system, without permission in writing from Lamp of Trismegistus. Reviewers may quote brief passages.

ISBN: 978-1-63118-452-9

Theosophical Classics

Other Books in this Series and Related Titles

Arcane Formulas or Mental Alchemy
William Walker Atkinson (978-1-63118-459-8)

The Machinery of the Mind by Dion Fortune (978-1-63118-451-2)

Crystal Vision Through Crystal Gazing by Achad (978-1-63118-455-0)

History, Analysis and Secret Tradition of the Tarot
by Manly P. Hall, A. E. Waite &c (978-1-63118-445-1)

Plato and Platonism and Related Esoteric Essays
by Helena P. Blavatsky & others (978-1-63118-432-1)

The Gospel of the Nativity of Mary by St. Matthew (978-1-63118-448-2)

The Mysteries of Freemasonry & the Druids
by Albert G. Mackey, Manly P. Hall &c (978-1-63118-444-4)

Essays on the Esoteric Tradition of Karma by William Q. Judge, Helena P. Blavatsky and Annie Besant (978-1-63118-426-0)

Magical Essays and Instructions by Florence Farr (978-1-63118-418-5)

The Secrets of Enoch by Enoch (978-1-63118-449-9)

Alchemy in the Nineteenth Century
by Helena P. Blavatsky (978-1-63118-446-8)

The Rosicrucian Chemical Marriage
by Christian Rosenkreuz (978-1-63118-458-1)

The Kabbalah of Masonry & Related Writings
by W. W. Westcott, Eliphas Levi &c (978-1-63118-453-6)

Freemasonry and the Egyptian Mysteries
by C. W. Leadbeater (978-1-63118-456-7)

Audio Versions are also Available on Audible and iTunes

Table of Contents

Introduction...7

Part I: *What It Is*...9

Part II: *How Is It Known*...11

Part III: *The Method of Observation*...15

Part IV: *General Principles*...19

Part V: *The Three Great Truths*...21

Part VI: *Advantages Gained From This Knowledge*...25

Part VII: *The Deity*...29

Part VIII: *The Divine Scheme*...33

Part IX: *The Constitution of Man*...37

Part X: *The True Man*...43

Part XI: *Reincarnation*...47

Part XII: *The Wider Outlook*...55

Part XIII: *Death*...59

Part XIV: *Man's Past and Future*...69

Part XV: *Cause and Effect*...75

Part XVI: *What Theosophy Does For Us*...81

Introduction

The Theosophical movement of the late nineteenth century provided the world with an extensive canon of literature related to a wide variety of esoteric subjects. Theosophical publications were proliferous, producing thousands of articles on such subjects as mysticism, astral projection, Rosicrucianism, Greek philosophy, alchemy, Qabalah, Hinduism and Buddhism, Hermeticism and so on. Throughout this material, the unifying factor was always altruism and the concept of a Universal Brotherhood. Readers eagerly consumed these new ideas; however, with the passage of time, challenging world events, new pass-times and the ever-changing interests of our society, many of these works have fallen to the wayside and become nearly forgotten.

Lamp of Trismegistus is doing its part to help preserve humanity's spiritual history, by making some of these classics available to those students who are seeking to unearth the knowledge of these ancient colossi. As such, Lamp of Trismegistus offers its readers highlights of esoteric study, culled from a variety of authors and viewpoints, with the hope bringing education back into the forefront of our theosophical and spiritual lives. So, be sure to check out other titles in our *Theosophical Classics* collection as well as our *Foundations of Freemasonry Series*, *Esoteric Classics*, *Occult Fiction*, *Supernatural Fiction*, *Paranormal Classics* and our *Christian Apocrypha Series*, and don't be afraid to let a little altruism into your own heart or even into your inner sanctum. You can also download the audio versions of most of these titles from iTunes or Audible for learning on the go.

PART I:
WHAT IT IS

For many a year, men have been discussing arguing, enquiring about certain great basic truths – about the existence and the Nature of God, about His relation to man, and about the past and future of humanity. So radically have they differed on these points, and so bitterly have they assailed and ridiculed one another's beliefs, that there has come to be a firmly-rooted popular opinion that with regard to all these matters there is no certainty available – nothing but vague speculation amid a cloud of unsound deductions drawn from ill-established premises. And this in spite of the very definite, though frequently incredible, assertions made on these subjects on behalf of the various religions.

This popular opinion, though not unnatural under the circumstances, is entirely untrue. There are definite facts available – plenty of them. Theosophy gives them to us; but it offers them not (as religions do) as matters of faith, but as subjects for study. It is itself not a religion, but it bears to religions the same relation as did the ancient philosophies. It does not contradict them, but explains them. Whatever in any of them is unreasonable, it rejects as necessarily unworthy of the Deity and derogatory to Him; whatever is reasonable in each and all of them it takes up, explains and emphasizes, and thus combines all into one harmonious whole.

It holds that truth on all these most important points is attainable – that there is a great body of knowledge about them already existing. It considers all the various religions as statements of that truth from different points of view; since, though they differ much as to nomenclature and as to articles of belief, they all agree as to the only matter which are of real importance – the kind of life which a good man should lead, the qualities which he must develop, the vices which he must avoid. On these practical points the teaching is identical in Hinduism and Buddhism, in Zoroasterianism and Mohammadanism, in Judaism and Christianity.

Theosophy may be described to the outside world as an intelligent theory of the universe. Yet for those who have studied it, it is not theory, but fact; for it is a definite science, capable of being studied, and its teachings are verifiable by investigation and experiment for those who are willing to take the trouble to qualify themselves for such enquiry. It is a statement of the great facts of Nature so far as they are known – an outline of the scheme of our corner of the universe.

PART II:
HOW IS IT KNOWN

How did this scheme become known, some may ask; by whom was it discovered? We cannot speak of it as discovered, for in truth it has always been known to mankind, though sometimes temporarily forgotten in certain parts of the world. There has always existed a certain body of highly developed men – men not of any one nation, but of all the advanced nations – who have held it in its fullness; and there has always been pupils of these men, who were specially studying it, while its broad principles have always been known in the outer world. This body of highly-developed men exists now, as in past ages, and Theosophical teaching is published to the Western world at their instigation, and through a few of their pupils.

Those who are ignorant have sometimes clamorously insisted that, if this be so, these truths ought to have been published long ago; and most unjustly they accuse the possessors of such knowledge of undue reticence in withholding them from the world at large. They forget that all who really sought these truths have always been able to find them, and that it is only now that we are in the Western world are truly beginning to seek.

For many centuries Europe was content to live, for the most part, in the grossest superstition; and when reaction at last set in from the absurdity and bigotry of those beliefs, it brought a period of atheism, which was just as conceited and bigoted in another direction. So that it is really only now that some of the humbler and more reasonable of our people are beginning to admit that they know nothing, and to enquire whether there is not real information available somewhere.

Though these reasonable enquirers are as yet a small minority, the Theosophical Society has been founded in order to draw them together, and its books are put before the public so that those who will, may read, mark, learn, and inwardly digest these great truths. Its mission is not to force its teaching upon reluctant minds, but simply to offer it, so that those may take it who feel the need for it. We are not in the least under the delusion of the poor arrogant missionary, who dares to condemn to an unpleasant eternity everyone who will not pronounce his little provincial shibboleth; we are perfectly aware that all will at last be well for those who cannot as yet see their way to accept the truth, as well as for those who receive it with avidity.

But the knowledge of this truth has, for us and for thousands of others, made life easier to bear and death easier to face; and it is simply the wish to share these benefits with our fellow men that urges us to devote ourselves to writing and lecturing on these subjects. The broad outlines of the great truths have been widely known in the world for thousands of years, and are so known in the present day. It is only we in the West who, in our incredible self-sufficiency, have remained ignorant of them, and scoffed at any fragment of them which may have come in our way.

As in the case of any other science, so in this science of the soul, full details are known only to those who devote their lives to its pursuit. The men who fully know – those who are called Adepts – have patiently developed within themselves the powers necessary for perfect observation. For in this respect there is a difference between the methods of occult investigation and those of the more modern form of science; this latter devotes all its energy to the improvement of its instruments, while the former aims rather at development of the observer.

PART III:
THE METHOD OF OBSERVATION

The detail of this development would take up more space than can be devoted to it in a preliminary manual such as this. The whole scheme will be found fully explained in other Theosophical works; for the moment let it suffice to say that it is entirely a question of vibration. All information which reaches a man from the world without, reaches him by means of vibration of some sort, whether it be through the senses of sight, hearing or touch. Consequently, if a man is able to make himself sensitive to additional vibrations he will acquire additional information; he will become what is commonly called "clairvoyant."

This word, as commonly used, means nothing more than a slight extension of normal vision; but it is possible for a man to become more and more sensitive to the subtler vibrations, until his consciousness, acting through many developed faculties, functions freely in new and higher ways. He will then find new worlds of subtler matter opening up before him, though in reality they are only new portions of the world he already knows.

He learns in this way that a vast unseen universe exists round him during his whole life, and that it is constantly affecting him in many ways, even though he remains blindly unconscious of it. But when he develops faculties whereby he can sense these other worlds, it becomes possible for him to observe them scientifically, to repeat his observations many times, to compare them with those of others, to tabulate them, and draw deductions from them.

All this has been done – not once, but thousands of times. The Adepts of whom I spoke have done this to the fullest possible extent, but many efforts along the same line have been made by our own Theosophical students. The result of our investigations has been not only to verify much of the information given to us at the outset by those Adepts, but also to explain and amplify it very considerably.

The sight of this usually unseen portion of our world at once brings to our knowledge a vast body of entirely new facts which are of the very deepest interest. It gradually solves for us many of the most difficult problems of life; it clears up for us many mysteries so that we now see them to have been mysteries to us for so long, only because heretofore we saw so small a part of the facts, because we were looking at the various matters from below, and as isolated and unconnected fragments, instead of rising above them to a standpoint whence they are comprehensible as parts of a mighty whole.

It settles in a moment many questions which have been much disputed – such, for example, as that of the continued existence of man after death. It affords us the true explanation of all the wildly impossible statements made by the churches about heaven, hell and purgatory; it dispels our ignorance and removes our fear of the unknown by supplying us with a rational and orderly scheme. What this scheme is I will now endeavor to explain.

PART IV:
GENERAL PRINCIPLES

It is my desire to make this statement of Theosophy as clear and readily comprehensible as possible, and for this reason I shall at every point give broad principles only, referring those who wish for detailed information to larger books, or to monographs upon particular subjects. I hope at the end of each chapter of this little treatise to give a list of such books as should be consulted by those who desire to go more deeply into this most fascinating system.

I shall begin then, by a statement of the most striking of the broad general principles which emerge as a result of Theosophical study. There may be those who find here matter which is incredible to them, or matter which runs entirely contrary to their preconceived ideas. If that be so, then I would ask such men to remember that I am not putting this forward as a theory – as a metaphysical speculation or a pious opinion of my own – but as a definite scientific fact proved and examined over and over again, not only by myself, but many others also.

Furthermore, I claim that it is a fact which may be verified at first hand by any person who is willing to devote the time and trouble necessary to fit himself for the investigation. I am not offering to the reader a creed to be swallowed like a pill; I am trying to set before him a system to study, and above all, a life to live. I ask no blind faith from him; I simply suggest to him the consideration of the Theosophical teaching as a hypothesis, though to me it is no hypothesis, but a living fact.

If he finds it more satisfactory than others which have been presented to him, if it seems to him to solve more of the problems of life, to answer a greater number of the questions which inevitably arise for thinking man, then he will pursue its study further, and will find in it, I hope and believe, the same ever-increasing satisfaction and joy that I have myself found.

If on the other hand, he thinks some other system preferable, no harm is done; he has simply learnt something of the tenets of a body of men with whom he is as yet unable to agree. I have sufficient faith in it myself to believe that, sooner or later, a time will come when he will agree with them – when he also will know what we know.

PART V:
THE THREE GREAT TRUTHS

In one of our earliest Theosophical books it was written that there are three truths which are absolute and cannot be lost, but yet may remain silent for lack of speech. They are as great as life itself, and yet as simple as the simplest mind of man. I can hardly do better than paraphrase these for the greatest of my general principles.

I will then give some corollaries which follow naturally from them, and then, thirdly, some of the more prominent of the advantageous results which necessarily attend this definite knowledge. Having thus outlined the scheme in tabular form, I will take it up point by point, and endeavor to offer such elementary explanations as come within the scope of this little introductory book.

God exists, and He is good. He is the great life-giver who dwells within us and without us, is undying and eternally beneficent. He is not heard, nor seen, nor touched, yet is perceived by the man who desires perception.

Man is immortal, and his future is one whose glory and splendor have no limit.

A Divine law of absolute justice rules the world, so that each man is in truth his own judge, the dispenser of glory or gloom to himself, the decreer of his life, his reward, his punishment.

To each of these great truths are attached certain others, subsidiary and explanatory.

From the first of them it follows:-

That, in spite of appearance, all things are definitely and intelligently moving together for good; that all circumstances, however untoward they may seem, are in reality exactly what are needed; that everything around us tends, not to hinder us, but to help us, if it is only understood.

That since the whole scheme thus tends to man's benefit, clearly it is his duty to learn to understand it.

That when he thus understands it, it is also his duty intelligently to co-operate in this scheme.

From the second great truth it follows:-

That the true man is a soul, and that this body is only an appanage.

That he must therefore, regard everything from the standpoint of the soul, and that in every case when an internal struggle takes place he must realize his identity with the higher and not with the lower.

That what we commonly call his life is only one day in his true and larger life.

That death is a matter of far less importance than is usually supposed, since it is by no means the end of life, but merely the passage from one stage of it to another.

That man has an immense evolution behind him, the study of which is most fascinating, interesting and instructive.

That he has also a splendid evolution before him, the study of which will be even more fascinating and instructive.

That there is an absolute certainty of final attainment for every human soul, no matter how far he may have seemed to have strayed from the path of evolution.

From the third great truth it follows:-

That every thought, word, or action produces its definite result – not a reward or a punishment imposed from without, but a result inherent in the action itself, definitely connected with it in the relation of cause and effect, these being really but two inseparable parts of one whole.

That it is both the duty and interest of man to study this divine law closely, so that he will be able to adapt himself to it and to use it, as we use other great laws of nature.

That it is necessary for man to attain perfect control over himself, so that he may guide his life intelligently in accordance with this law.

PART VI:
ADVANTAGES GAINED FROM THIS KNOWLEDGE

When this knowledge is fully assimilated, it changes the aspect of life so completely that it would be impossible for me to tabulate all the advantages which flow from it. I can only mention a few of the principal lines along which this change is produced, and the reader's own thought will, no doubt, supply some of the endless ramifications which are their necessary consequence.

But it must be understood that no vague knowledge will be sufficient. Such belief as most men accord to the assertions of their religions will be quite useless, since it produces no practical effect in their lives. But if we believe in these truths as we do in the other laws of nature – as we believe that fire burns and that water drowns – then the effect that they produce in our lives is enormous.

For our belief in the laws of Nature is sufficiently real to induce us to order our lives in accordance with it. Believing that fire burns, we take every precaution to avoid fire; believing that water drowns, we avoid going into water too deep for us unless we can swim.

Now these beliefs are so definite and real to us because they are founded on knowledge and illustrated by daily experience; and the beliefs of the Theosophical student are equally real and definite to him for exactly the same reason. And that is why we find following from them the results now to be described:

We gain a rational comprehension of life – we know how we should live and why, and we learn that life is worth living when properly understood.

We learn how to govern ourselves, and therefore how to develop ourselves.

We learn how best to help those whom we love, how to make ourselves useful to all with whom we come into contact, and ultimately to the whole human race.

We learn to view everything from the wider philosophical standpoint – never from the petty and purely personal side.

Consequently:

The troubles of life are no longer so large for us.

We have no sense of injustice in connection with our surroundings or our destiny.

We are altogether freed from the fear of death.

Our grief in connection with the death of those whom we love is very greatly mitigated.

We gain a totally different view of life after death, and we understand its place in our evolution.

We are altogether free from religious fears or worry, either for ourselves or for our friends – fears as to the salvation of the soul, for example.

We are no longer troubled by uncertainty as to our future fate, but live in perfect serenity and perfect fearlessness.

Now let us take these points in detail, and endeavor briefly to explain them.

PART VII: THE DEITY

When we lay down the existence of God as the first and greatest of our principles, it becomes necessary for us to define the sense in which we employ that much abused, yet mighty word. We try to redeem it from the narrow limits imposed on it by the ignorance of undeveloped men, and to restore to it the splendid conception – splendid, though so infinitely below the reality – given to it by the founders of religions. And we distinguish between God as the Infinite Existence, and the manifestation of this Supreme Existence as a revealed God, evolving and guiding a universe.

Only to this limited manifestation should the term "a personal God" be applied. God in Himself is beyond the bounds of the personality, is "in all and through all," and indeed is all; and of the Infinite, the Absolute, the All, we can only say "He is."

For all practical purposes we need not go further than that marvelous and glorious manifestation of Him (a little less entirely beyond our comprehension) the great Guiding Force or deity of our own solar system, whom philosophers have called the Logos. Of Him is true all that we have ever heard predicted of God – all that is good, that is – not the blasphemous conceptions sometimes put forward, ascribing to Him human vices.

But all that has ever been said of the love, the wisdom, the power the patience and compassion, the omniscience, the omnipresence, the omnipotence –all of this, and much more, is true of the Logos of our system. Verily "in Him we live and move and have our being," not as a poetical expression, but (strange as it may seem) as a definite scientific fact; and so when we speak of the deity our first thought is naturally of the Logos.

We do not vaguely hope that He may be; we do not even believe as a matter of faith that He is; we simply know it as we know that the sun shines, for to the trained and developed clairvoyant investigator this Mighty existence is a definite certainty. Not that any merely human development can enable us directly to see Him, but that unmistakable evidence of His action and His purpose surrounds us on every side as we study the life of the unseen world, which is in reality only the higher part of this.

Here we meet the explanation of a dogma which is common to all religions – that of the Trinity. Incomprehensible as many of the statements made on this subject in our creeds may seem to the ordinary reader, they become significant and luminous when the truth is understood. As He shows Himself to us in His work, the Solar Logos is undoubtedly triple – three yet one, as religion has long ago told us; and as much of the explanation of this apparent mystery as the intellect of man at its present stage can grasp will be found in the books presently to be mentioned.

That He is within us as well as without us, or, in other words, that man himself is in essence divine, is another great truth which, though those who are blind to all but the outer and lower world may still argue about it, is an absolute certainty to the student of the higher side of life. Of the constitution of man's soul and its various vehicles we shall speak under the heading of the second of truths; suffice it for the moment to note that the inherent divinity is a fact, and that in it resides the assurance of the ultimate return of every human being to the divine level.

PART VIII:
THE DIVINE SCHEME

Perhaps none of our postulates will present greater difficulty to the average mind than the first corollary to the first great truth. Looking round us in daily life we see so much of the storm and stress, the sorrow and suffering, so much that looks like the triumph of evil over good, that it seems almost impossible to suppose that all this apparent confusion is in reality part of an ordered process. Yet this is the truth, and can be seen to be the truth so soon as we escape from the dust-cloud raised by the struggle in the outer world, and look upon it all from the vantage ground of the fuller knowledge and the inner peace.

Then the real motion of the complex machinery becomes apparent. Then it is seen that what have seemed to be countercurrents of evil prevailing against the stream of progress are merely trifling eddies into which for the moment a little water may turn aside, or tiny whirlpools on the surface, in which part of the water appears for the moment to be running backwards.

But all the time the mighty river is sweeping steadily on its appointed course, bearing the superficial whirlpools along with it. Just so the great stream of evolution is moving evenly on its way, and what seems to us so terrible a tempest is the merest ruffling of its surface. Another analogy, very beautifully worked out is given in Mr. C. H. Hinton's *Scientific Romances*, vol. 1.

Truly, as our third great truth tells us, absolute justice is meted out to all, and so, in whatever circumstances a man finds himself, he knows that he himself and none other has provided them; but he may also know much more than this. He may rest assured that under the action of evolutionary law matters are so arranged as to give him the best possible opportunity for developing within himself those qualities which he most needs.

His circumstances are by no means necessarily those that he would have chosen for himself, but they are exactly what he deserved; and subject only to that consideration of his deserts (which frequently impose serious limitations), they are those best adapted for his progress. They may provide him with all sorts of difficulties, but these are offered only in order that he may learn to surmount them, and thereby develop within himself courage, determination, patience, perseverance, or whatever other quality he may lack. Men often speak as though the forces of nature were conspiring against them, whereas as a matter of fact, if they would but understand it, everything about them is carefully calculated to assist them on their upward way.

That, since there is a Divine scheme, it is man's part to try and understand it, is a proposition which surely needs no argument. Even were it only from motives of self-interest, those who have to live under a certain set of conditions would do well to familiarize themselves with them; and when a man's objects in life become altruistic it is still more necessary for him to comprehend, in order that he may help the more effectually.

It is undoubtedly part of this plan for man's evolution that he himself should intelligently co-operate in it as soon as he has developed sufficient intelligence to grasp it and sufficient good feeling to wish to aid. But indeed this Divine scheme is so wonderful and so beautiful that, when once a man sees it, nothing else is possible for him than to throw all his energies into the effort to become a worker in it, no matter how humble may be the part which he has to sustain.

For fuller information on the subjects of this chapter the reader is referred to Mrs. Besant's *Esoteric Christianity* and *Ancient Wisdom*, and to my own little book on *The Christian Creed*. Much light is also thrown on these conceptions from the Greek standpoint in Mr. G. R. S. Mead's *Orpheus*, and from the Gnostic-Christian in his *Fragments Of A Faith Forgotten*.

PART IX:
THE CONSTITUTION OF MAN

The astounding practical materialism to which we have been reduced in this country can hardly be more clearly shown than it is by the expressions that we employ in common life. We speak quite ordinarily of man as having a soul, of "saving" our souls, and so on, evidently regarding the physical body as the real man and the soul as a mere appanage, a vague something to be considered as property of the body.

With an idea so little defined as this, it can hardly be a matter of surprise that many people go a little further along the same lines, and doubt whether this vague something exists at all. So it would seem that the ordinary man is very often quite uncertain whether he possesses a soul or not; still less does he know that the soul is immortal. That he should remain in this pitiable condition of ignorance seems strange, for there is a very great deal of evidence available even in the outer world, to show that man has an existence quite apart from his body, capable of being carried on at a distance from it while it is living, and entirely without it when it is dead.

Until we have entirely rid ourselves of this extraordinary delusion that the body is the man, it is quite impossible that we should at all appreciate the real facts of the case. A little investigation immediately shows us that the body is only a vehicle by means of which the man manifests himself in connection with this particular type of gross matter out of which our visible world is built.

Furthermore, it shows that other and subtler types of matter exist – not only the ether admitted by modern science as interpenetrating all known substances, but other types of matter which interpenetrate ether in turn, and are as much finer than ether as it is than solid matter. The question will naturally occur to the reader as to how it will be possible for man to become conscious of the existence of types of matter so wonderfully fine, so minutely subdivided. The answer is that he can become conscious of them in the same way as he becomes conscious of the lower matter – by receiving vibrations from them.

And he is enabled to receive vibrations from them by reason of the fact that he possesses matter of these finer types as part of himself – that just as his body of dense matter is his vehicle for perceiving and communicating with the world of dense matter, so does the finer matter within him constitute for him a vehicle by means of which he can perceive and communicate with the world of finer matter which is imperceptible to the grosser physical senses.

This is by no means a new idea. It will be remembered that St. Paul remarks that "there is a natural body, and there is a spiritual body," and that he furthermore refers to both the soul and the spirit in man, by no means employing the two synonymously, as is so often ignorantly done at the present day. It speedily becomes evident that man is a far more complex being than is ordinarily supposed; that not only is he a spirit within a soul but that this soul has various vehicles of different degrees of density, the physical body being only one, and the lowest of them.

These various vehicles may all be described as bodies in relation to their respective levels of matter. It might be said that there exist around us a series of worlds one within the other (by inter-penetration), and that man possesses a body for each of these worlds, by means of which he may observe it and live in it. He learns by degrees how to use these various bodies, and in that way gains a much more complete idea of the great complex world in which he lives; for all these other inner worlds are in reality still part of it.

In this way he comes to understand very many things which before seemed mysterious to him; he ceases to identify himself with his bodies, and learns that they are only vestures which he may put off and resume or change without being himself in the least affected thereby. Once more we must repeat that all this by no means metaphysical speculation or pious opinion, but definite scientific fact thoroughly well-known experimentally to those who have studied Theosophy.

Strange as it may seem to many, to find precise statements taking the place of hypothesis upon questions such as these, I am speaking here of nothing that is not known by direct and constantly repeated observation to a large number of students. Assuredly "we know whereof we speak," not by faith but by experiment, and therefore we speak with confidence. To these inner worlds or different levels of nature we usually give the name of planes. We speak of the visible world as "the physical plane," though under that name we include also the gases and various grades of ether.

To the next stage of materiality the name of "the astral plane" was given by the medieval alchemists (who were well aware of its existence), and we have adopted their title. Within this exists another world of still finer matter, of which we speak as "the mental plane," because of its matter is composed what is commonly called the mind in man. There are other still higher planes, but I need not trouble the reader with designations for them, since we are at present dealing only with man's manifestation in the lower worlds.

It must always be born in mind that all these worlds are in no way removed from us in space. In fact, they all occupy exactly the same space, and are all equally about us always. At the moment our consciousness is focused in and working through our physical brain, and thus we are conscious only of the physical world, and not even of the whole of that. But we have only to learn to focus that consciousness in one of these higher vehicles, and at once the physical fades from our view, and we see instead the world of matter which corresponds to the vehicle used.

Recollect that all matter is in essence the same. Astral matter does not differ in its nature from physical matter anymore than ice differs in its nature from steam. It is simply the same thing in a different condition. Physical matter may become astral, or astral may become mental, if only it be sufficiently subdivided, and caused to vibrate with the proper degree of rapidity.

PART X:
THE TRUE MAN

What, then is the true man? He is in truth an emanation from the Logos, a spark of the Divine fire. The spirit within him is of the very essence of the Deity, and that spirit wears his soul as a vesture – a vesture which encloses and individualizes it, and seems to our limited vision to separate it for a time from the rest of the Divine Life. The story of the original formation of the soul of man, and of the enfolding of the spirit within it, is a beautiful and interesting one, but too long for inclusion in a merely elementary work like this. It may be found in full detail in those of our books which deal with this part of the doctrine.

Suffice it here to say that all three aspects of the Divine Life have their part in its inception, and that its formation is the culmination of that mighty sacrifice of the Logos in descending into matter, which has been called the Incarnation. Thus the baby soul is born; and just as it is "made in the image of God" – threefold in aspect, as He is, and threefold in manifestation, as He is also – so is its method of evolution also a reflection of His descent into matter. The Divine Spark contains within it all potentiality, but it is only through long ages of evolution that all its possibilities can be realized.

The appointed method for the evolution of the man's latent qualities seems to be by learning to vibrate in response to the impacts from without. But at the level where he finds himself (that of the higher mental plane) the vibrations are far too fine to awaken this response at present; he must begin with those that are coarser and stronger, and having awakened his dormant sensibilities by their means he will gradually grow more and more sensitive until he is capable of perfect response at all levels to all possible rates of vibration.

That is the material aspect of his progress; but regarded subjectively, to be able to respond to all vibrations means to be perfect in sympathy and compassion. And that is exactly the condition of the developed man –the adept, the spiritual teacher, the Christ. It needs the development within him of all the qualities which go to make up the perfect man; and this is the real work of his long life in matter. In this chapter we have brushed the surface of many subjects of extreme importance. Those who wish to study them further will find many Theosophical books to help them.

On the constitution of man, we would refer readers to Mrs. Besant's works, *Man and His Bodies*, *The Self And Its Sheaths*, and *The Seven Principles Of Man*, and, also my own book, Man, *Visible And Invisible*, in which will be found many illustrations of the different vehicles of man as they appear to the clairvoyant sight. On the use of the inner faculties refer to *Clairvoyance*.

On the formation and evolution of the soul to Mrs. Besant's *Birth and Evolution of the Soul*, Mr. Sinnett's *Growth of the Soul*, and my own *Christian Creed* and *Man, Visible and Invisible*.

On the spiritual evolution of man, Mrs. Besant's *In the Outer Court* and *The Path of Discipleship*, and the concluding chapters of my own little book, *Invisible Helpers*.

PART XI: REINCARNATION

Since the finer movements cannot at first affect the soul, he has to draw round him vestures of grosser matter through which the heavier vibrations can play; and so he takes upon himself successively the mental body, the astral body, and the physical body. This is a birth or incarnation –the commencement of a physical life. During that life all kinds of experiences come to him through his physical body, and from them he should learn some lessons and develop some qualities in himself.

After a time he begins to withdraw into himself, and puts off by degrees the vestures which he has assumed. The first of these to drop is the physical body, and his withdrawal from that is what we call death. It is not the end of his activities, as we so ignorantly suppose; nothing could be further from the fact. He is simply withdrawing from one effort, bearing back with him its results; and after a certain period of comparative repose he will make another effort of the same kind.

Thus, as has been said, what we ordinarily call his life is only one day in the real and wider life – a day at school, during which he learns certain lessons. But inasmuch as one short life of seventy or eighty years at most is not enough to give him an opportunity of learning all the lessons which this wonderful and beautiful world has to teach, and inasmuch as God means him to learn them all in His own good time, it is necessary that he should come back again many times, and live through many of these schooldays that we call lives, in different classes and under different circumstances, until all the lessons are learned; and then this lower schoolwork will be over, and he will pass to something higher and more glorious – the true divine lifework for which all this earthly school-life is fitting him.

That is what is called the doctrine of reincarnation or rebirth – a doctrine which was widely known in the ancient civilizations, and is even today held by the majority of the human race.

Of it Hume has written:-

"What is incorruptible must also be ungenerable. The soul, therefore, if immortal, existed before our birth…..The metempsychosis is, therefore, the only system of this kind that Philosophy can hearken to." (*Hume. "Essay on Immortality," London, 1875*).

Writing of the theories of metempsychosis in India and Greece, Max Muller says:- "There is something underlying them all which, if expressed in less mythological language, may stand the severest test of philosophical examination." (*Max Muller, 'Theosophy or Psychological Religion,' p. 22, 1895 ed.*)

In his last and posthumous work this great Orientalist again refers to this doctrine, and expresses his personal belief in it.

And Huxley writes: - "Like the doctrine of evolution itself, that of transmigration has its roots in the world of reality; and it may claim such support as the great argument from analogy is capable of supplying." (*Huxley, "Evolution and Ethics," p. 61, 1895 ed.*)

So it will be seen that modern as well as ancient writers recognize this hypothesis as one deserving of the most serious consideration.

It must not for a moment be confounded with a theory held by the ignorant, that it was possible for a soul which had reached humanity in its evolution to re-become that of an animal. No such retrogression is within the limits of possibility; when once man comes into existence – a human soul, inhabiting what we call in our books a causal body – he can never again fall back into what is in truth a lower kingdom of nature, whatever mistakes he may make or however he may fail to take advantage of his opportunities. If he is idle in the school of life, he may need to take the same lesson over and over again before he has really learned it , but still on the whole progress is steady, even though it may often be slow. A few years ago the essence of this doctrine was prettily put thus in one of the magazines: -

"A boy went to school. He was very little. All that he knew he had drawn in with his mother's milk. His teacher (who was God) placed him in the lowest class, and gave him these lessons to learn: Thou shalt not kill. Thou shalt do no hurt to any living thing. Thou shalt not steal. So the man did not kill; but he was cruel, and he stole, - At the end of the day (when his beard was grey – when the night was come) his teacher (who was God) said – Thou hast learned not to kill. But the other lessons thou hast not learned. Come back tomorrow."

"On the morrow he came back, a little boy, and his teacher (who was God) put him in a class a little higher, and gave him these lessons to learn: Thou shalt do no hurt to any living thing. Thou shalt not steal. Thou shalt not cheat. So the man did no hurt to any living thing; but he stole and he cheated. And at the end of the day – when his beard was grey – when the night was come – his teacher (who was god) said: Thou hast learned to be merciful. But the other lessons thou hast not learned. Come back tomorrow."

"Again, on the morrow, he came back, a little boy. And his teacher (who was God) put him in a class yet a little higher, and gave these lessons to learn: Thou shalt not steal. Thou shalt not cheat. Thou shalt not covet. So the man did not steal; but he cheated, and he coveted. And at the end of the day – (when his beard was grey –when night was come) his teacher (who was God) said: Thou hast learned not to steal. But the other lessons thou hast not learned. Come back, my child, tomorrow."

"This is what I have read in the faces of men and women, in the book of the world, and in the scroll of the heavens, which is writ in the stars." (*Berry Benson, in* The Century Magazine, *May 1894*).

I must not fill my pages with the many unanswerable arguments in favor of this doctrine of reincarnation; they are set forth very fully in our literature by a far abler pen than mine. Here I will say only this. Life presents us with many problems which, on any other hypothesis than this of reincarnation, seem utterly insoluble; this great truth does explain them, and therefore holds the field until another more satisfactory hypothesis can be found. Like the rest of the teaching, this is not a Hypothesis, but a matter of direct knowledge for many of us; but naturally our knowledge is not proof to others.

Yet good men and true have been sorrowfully forced to admit that they were unable to reconcile the state of affairs which exists in the world around us with the theory that God was both almighty and all-loving. They felt, when they looked upon all the heartbreaking sorrow and suffering, that either He was not almighty, and could not prevent it, or He was not all-loving, and did not care. In Theosophy we hold with determined conviction that He is both almighty and all-loving, and we reconcile with that certainty the existing facts of life by means of this basic doctrine of reincarnation. Surely the only hypothesis which allows us reasonably to recognize the perfection of power and love in the Deity is one which is worthy of careful examination.

For we understand that our present life is not our first, but that each have behind us a long line of lives, by means of which we have evolved from the condition of primitive man to our present position. Assuredly in these past lives we shall have done both good and evil, and from every one of our actions a definite proportion of result must have followed under the inexorable law of justice. From the good follows always happiness and further opportunity; from the evil follows always sorrow and limitation.

So, if we find ourselves limited in any way, the limitation is of our own making, or is merely due to the youth of the soul; if we have sorrow and suffering to endure, we ourselves alone are responsible. The manifold and complex destinies of men answer with rigid exactitude to the balance between the good and evil of their previous actions; and all is moving onward under the divine order towards the final consummation of glory.

There is perhaps, no Theosophical teaching to which more violent objection is made than this great truth of reincarnation; yet it is in reality a most comforting doctrine. For it gives us time for the progress which lies before – time and opportunity to become "perfect." Objectors chiefly found their protest on the fact that they have had so much trouble and sorrow in this life that they will not listen to any suggestion that it may be necessary to go through it all again. But this is obviously not argument; we are in search of truth, and when it is found we must not shrink from it, whether it be pleasant or unpleasant, though, as a matter of fact, as said above, reincarnation rightly understood is profoundly comforting.

Again, people often enquire why, if we have had so many previous lives, we do not remember any of them. Put briefly, the answer to this is that some people do remember them; and the reason why the majority do not is because their consciousness is still focused in one or other of the lower sheaths. That sheath cannot be expected to recollect previous incarnations, because it has not had any; and the soul, which has, is not yet fully conscious on its own plane. But the memory of all the past is stored within the soul, and expresses itself here in the innate qualities with which the child is born; and when the man has evolved sufficiently to be able to focus his consciousness there instead of only in lower vehicles the entire history of that real and wider life will be open before him like a book.

The whole of this question is fully and beautifully worked out in Mrs. Besant's manual on *Reincarnation*, Dr, Jerome Anderson's *Reincarnation* and in the chapters on that subject in *The Ancient Wisdom*, to which the attention of the reader is specially directed.

PART XII:
THE WIDER OUTLOOK

A little thought will soon show us what a radical change is introduced into the life of the man who realizes that his physical life is nothing but a day at school, and that his physical body is merely a temporary vesture assumed for the purpose of learning through it. He sees at once that this purpose of "learning the lesson" is the only one of any importance, and that the man who allows himself to be diverted from that purpose by any consideration is acting with inconceivable stupidity.

To him who knows the truth, the life of the ordinary person devoted exclusively to physical objects, to the pursuit of wealth and fame, appears the merest child's play – a senseless sacrifice of all that is really worth having for a few moment's gratification of the lower parts of man's nature. The student "sets his affection on things above, and not on things of the earth," not only because he sees this to be a right course of action, but because he realizes very clearly the valuelessness of these things of earth. He always tries to take the higher point of view, for he sees that the lower is utterly unreliable – that the lower desires and feelings gather round him like a dense fog, and make it impossible for him to see anything clearly from that level.

Yet even when he is thoroughly convinced that the higher course is always the right one, and when he is fully determined to follow it, he will nevertheless sometimes encounter very strong temptations to take the lower course, and will be sensible of a great struggle within him. He will discover that there is "a law of the members warring against the law of the mind," as St. Paul says, so that "those things that I would, I do not, and the thing which I would not, that I do."

Now good religious people often make the most serious mistakes about this interior struggle which we have all felt to a greater or less extent. They usually accept one or two theories on the subject. Either they suppose that the lower promptings come from exterior tempting demons, or else they mourn over the terrible wickedness and blackness of their hearts, in that such fathomless evil still exists within them. Indeed, many of the best men and women go through a vast amount of totally unnecessary suffering on this account.

The first point to have clearly in mind if one wishes to understand this matter is that the lower desire is not in truth our desire at all. Nor is it the work of some demon trying to destroy our souls. It is true that there sometimes are evil entities which are attracted by the base thought in man, and intensify it by their action; but such entities are man-made, every one of them, and impermanent. They are merely artificial forms called into existence by the thought of other evil men, and they have a period of what seems almost like life, proportioned to the strength of the thought that created them.

But the undesirable prompting within us usually comes from quite another source. It has been mentioned how man draws round him vestures of matter at different levels, in order that he may descend into incarnation. But this matter is not dead matter (indeed, occult science teaches us that there is no such thing as dead matter anywhere), but it is instinct with life; though it is life at a stage of evolution much earlier than our own – so much earlier that it is still moving on a downward course into lower matter, instead of rising again out of lower matter into higher.

Consequently its tendency is always to press downwards towards the grosser material and the coarser vibrations which mean progress for it, but retrogression for us; and so it happens that the interest of the true man sometimes comes into collision with that of the living matter in some of his vehicles.

That is a very rough outline of the explanation of the curious internal strife that we sometimes feel – a strife which has suggested to the poetic minds the idea of good and evil angels in conflict over the soul of man. A more detailed account will be found in *The Astral Plane*. But in the meantime it is important that the man should realize that he is the higher force, always moving towards and battling for good, while this lower force is not he at all, but only an uncontrolled fragment of one of his lower vehicles. He must learn to control it, to dominate it absolutely, and to keep it in order; but he should not therefore, think of it as evil, but as an outpouring of the Divine power moving on its orderly course, though that course in this instance happens to be downwards into matter, instead of upwards and away from it, as ours is.

PART XIII:
DEATH

One of the most important practical results of a thorough comprehension of Theosophical truth is the entire change which is necessary brings about in our attitude towards death. It is impossible for us to calculate the vast amount of utterly unnecessary sorrow and terror and misery which mankind in the aggregate has suffered simply from its ignorance and superstition with regard to this one matter of death. There is among us a mass of false and foolish belief along this line which has worked untold evil in the past and is causing indescribable suffering in the present, and its eradication would be one of the greatest benefits that could be conferred upon the human race.

This benefit the Theosophical teaching at once confers on those who, from their study of philosophy in past lives, now find themselves able to accept it. It robs death forthwith of all its terror and much of its sorrow, and enables us to see it in its true proportions and to understand its place in the scheme of our evolution.

While death is considered as the end of life, as the gateway into a dim but fearful unknown country, it is not unnaturally regarded with much misgiving, if not with positive terror. Since, in spite of all religious teaching to the contrary this has been the view universally taken in the western world, many grisly horrors have sprung up around it, and have become matters of custom, thoughtlessly obeyed by many who should know better.

All the ghastly paraphernalia of woe – the mutes, the plumes, the black velvet, the crape, the mourning garments, the black-edged note paper –all these are nothing more than advertisements of ignorance on the part of those who employ them. The man who begins to understand what death is at once puts aside all this masquerade as childish folly, seeing that to mourn over the good fortune of his friend merely because it involves for himself the pain of apparent separation from that friend, becomes, as soon as it is recognized, a display of selfishness.

He cannot avoid feeling the wrench of the temporary separation, but he can avoid allowing his own pain to become a hindrance to the friend who has passed on. He knows that there can be no need to fear or to mourn over death, whether it comes to himself or to those whom he loves. It has come to them all often before, so that there is nothing unfamiliar about it. Instead of representing it as a ghastly king of terrors, it would be more accurate and more sensible to symbolize it as an angel bearing a golden key to admit us to the glorious realms of the higher life.

He realizes very definitely that life is continuous, and that the loss of the physical body is nothing more than the casting aside of a garment which in no way changes the real man who is the wearer of the garment. He sees that death is simply a promotion from a life which is more than half-physical to one which is wholly astral, and therefore very much superior. So, for himself he unfeignedly welcomes it, and when it comes to those whom he loves, he recognizes at once the great advantage for them, even though he cannot feel a certain amount of selfish regret that he should be temporarily separated from them.

But he knows also that this separation is in fact only apparent, and not real. He knows that the so-called dead are near him still, and that he has only to cast off temporarily his physical body in sleep, in order to stand side by side with them and commune with them as before. He sees clearly that the world is one and that the same Divine laws rule the whole of it, whether it be visible or invisible to the physical sight. Consequently he has no feeling of nervousness or strangeness in passing from one part of it to the other, and no sort of uncertainty as to what he will find on the other side of the veil.

The whole of the unseen world is so clearly and fully mapped out for him through the work of the Theosophical investigators that it is well known to him as the physical life, and thus he is prepared to enter upon it without hesitation whenever it may be best for his evolution. For full details of the various stages of this higher life we must refer the reader to the books specially devoted to this subject. It is sufficient here to say that the conditions into which the man passes are precisely those which the man passes are precisely those which he has made for himself. The thoughts and desires which he has encouraged within himself during earth-life take form as definite living entities hovering round him and reacting upon him until the energy which he poured into them is exhausted.

When such thoughts and desires have been powerful and persistently evil, the companions so created may indeed be terrible; but happily such cases form a very small minority among the dwellers in the astral world. The worst that the ordinary man of the world usually provides for himself after death is a useless and unutterably wearisome existence, void of all rational interests – the natural sequence of a life wasted in self-indulgence, triviality, and gossip here on earth.

To this weariness active suffering may under certain conditions be added. If a man during earth-life has allowed strong physical desire to obtain a mastery over him – if, for example, he has become a slave to such a vice as avarice, sensuality, or drunkenness – he has laid up for himself much purgatorial suffering after death. For in losing the physical body he in no way loses these desires and passions; they remain as vivid as ever – nay, they are even more active when they have no longer the heavy particles of dense matter to set in motion. What he does lose is the power to gratify these passions; so that they remain as torturing, gnawing desires, unsatisfied and unsatisfiable. It will be seen that this makes a very real hell for the unfortunate man, though of course only a temporary one, since in process of time such desires must burn themselves out, expending their energy in the very suffering which they produce.

A terrible fate, truly; yet there are two points which we should bear in mind with regard to it. First, that the man has not only brought it on himself, but has determined its intensity and its duration for himself. He has allowed this desire to reach a certain strength during earth-life, and now he has to meet it and control it. If during physical life he has made efforts to repress or check it, he will have just so much the less difficulty in conquering it now. He has created for himself the monster with which now he has to struggle; whatever strength his antagonist possesses is just what he has given it. Therefore, his fate is not imposed upon him from without, but is simply of his own making.

Secondly, the suffering which he thus brings upon himself is the only way of escape for him. If it were possible for him to avoid it, and to pass through the astral life without this gradual wearing away of the lower desires, what would be the result? Obviously that he would enter upon his next physical life entirely under the domination of these passions. He would be a born drunkard, a sensualist, a miser; and long before it would be possible to teach him that he ought to try to control such passions they would have grown far too strong for control – they would have enslaved him, body and soul, and so another life would be thrown away, another opportunity would be lost. He would enter thus upon a vicious circle from which there appears no escape, and his evolution would be indefinitely delayed.

The Divine scheme is not thus defective. The passion exhausts itself during the astral life, and the man returns to physical existence without it. True, the weakness of mind which allowed passion to dominate him is still there; true also, he has made for himself for this new life an astral body capable of expressing exactly the same passions as before, so that it would not be difficult for him to resume his old evil life. But the ego, the real man, has had a terrible lesson, and assuredly he will make every effort to prevent his lower manifestation from repeating that mistake, from falling again under the sway of that passion.

He has still the germs of it within him, but if he has deserved good and wise parents they will help to develop the good in him and check the evil, the germs will remain unfructified and will atrophy, and so in the next life after that they will not appear at all. So by slow degrees man conquers his evil qualities, and evolves virtues to replace them.

On the other hand, the man who is intelligent and helpful, who understands the conditions of this non-physical existence and takes the trouble to adapt himself to them and make the most of them, opening before him a splendid vista of opportunities both for acquiring fresh knowledge and for doing useful work. He discovers that life away from this dense body has a vividness and brilliancy to which all earthly enjoyment is as moonlight unto sunlight, and that through his clear knowledge and calm confidence the power of the endless life shines out upon all those around him.

He may become a center of peace and joy unspeakable to hundreds of his fellow men, and may do more good in a few years of that astral existence than ever he could have done in the longest physical life. He is well aware too, that there lies before him another and still grander stage of this wonderful post-mortem life. Just as by his desires and his lower thoughts he has made for himself the surroundings of his astral life, so has he by his higher thought and his nobler aspirations made for himself a life in the heaven-world.

For heaven is not a dream, but a living and glorious reality. Not a city far away beyond the stars, with gates of pearl and streets of gold, reserved for the habitation of a favored few, but a state of consciousness into which every man will pass during the interval between lives on earth. Not an eternal abiding-place truly, but a condition of bliss indescribable lasting through many centuries. Not even that alone. For although it contains the reality which underlies all the best and most spiritual ideas of heaven which have been propounded in various religions, yet it must by no means be considered from that view only.

It is a realm of nature which is of exceeding importance to us — a vast and splendid world of vivid life in which we are living now, as well as in the periods intervening between physical incarnations. It is only our lack of development, only the limitation imposed upon us by this robe of flesh, that prevents us from fully realizing that all glory of the brightest heaven is about us here and now, and that influences flowing from that world are ever playing upon us, if we will only understand and receive them.

Impossible as this may seem to the man of the world, it is the plainest of realities to the occultist; and to those who have not yet grasped this fundamental truth we can but repeat the advice given by the Buddhist teacher: - "Do not complain and cry and pray, but open your eyes and see." The light is all about you, if you would only cast the bandage from your eyes and look. It is so wonderful, so beautiful, so far beyond what any man has dreamt of or prayed for, and it is for ever and ever."

When the astral body, which is the vehicle of the lower thought and desire, has gradually been worn away and left behind, the man finds himself inhabiting that higher vehicle of finer matter which we have called the mental body. In this vehicle he is able to respond to the vibrations which reach him from the corresponding matter in the external world – the matter of the mental plane. His time of purgatory is over, the lower part of his nature has burnt itself away, and now there remain only the higher thoughts and aspirations which he has poured forth during earth-life.

These cluster round him, through the medium of which he is able to respond to certain types of vibration in this refined matter. These thoughts which surround him are the powers by which he draws upon the wealth of the heaven world. This mental plane is a reflection of the Divine Mind – a storehouse of infinite extent from which the person enjoying heaven is able to draw just according to the power of his own thoughts and aspirations generated during the physical and astral life.

All religions have spoken of the bliss of Heaven, yet few of them have put before us with sufficient clearness this leading idea which alone explains rationally how for all alike such bliss is possible – which is, the keynote of the conception – the fact that each man makes his own heaven by selection from the ineffable splendors of the Thought of God Himself. A man decides for himself both the length and the character of his heaven-life by the causes which he himself generates during his earth-life; therefore, he cannot but have exactly the amount which he has deserved and exactly the quality of joy which is best suited to his idiosyncrasies.

This is a world in which every being must, from the very fact of his consciousness there, be enjoying the highest spiritual bliss of which he is capable – a world whose power of response to his aspirations is limited only by his capacity to aspire. Further details as to the astral life will be found in the *Astral Plane*; the heaven life is described in *The Devachanic Plane*, and information about both is also given in *Death and After*, and in *The Other Side of Death*.

PART XIV:
MAN'S PAST AND FUTURE

When we have once grasped the fact that man has reached his present position through a long and varied series of lives, a question naturally arises in our minds as to how far we can obtain any information about this earlier evolution, which would obviously be of absorbing interest to us. Fortunately such information is available, not only by tradition, but also in another and much more certain way. I have so space here to dilate upon the marvels of psychometry, but must simply say that there is abundant evidence to show that nothing can happen without indelibly recording itself – that there exists a kind of memory of Nature from which can be recovered with absolute accuracy a true, full, and perfect picture of any scene or event since the world began.

Those to whom this subject is entirely new, and who consequently seek for evidence, should consult Dr. Buchanan's *Psychometry* or Professor Denton's *Soul of Things*; but all occult students are familiar with the possibility, and most of them with the method, of reading these records of the past. In essence this memory of Nature must be the Divine Memory, far away beyond human reach; but it is assuredly reflected into the lower planes so that, as far as events on these lower planes are concerned, it is recoverable by the trained intelligence of man.

All that passes before a mirror, for instance, is reflected on its surface, and to our dim eyes it seems that the images make no impression on that surface, but that each passes away and leaves no trace. Yet that may not be so; it is not difficult to imagine that an impression may be left, somewhat as the impression of every sound is left upon the sensitive cylinder of a phonograph; and it may be possible to recover the impression from the mirror just as it is recoverable from the phonograph.

The higher psychometry shows us that this not only may be so, but is so; and that not a mirror only, but any physical object, retains the impression of all that has happened within its sight, as it were. We have thus at our disposal a faultlessly accurate method of arriving at the earlier history of our world and of mankind, and in this way much that is of the most entrancing interest can be observed in every detail, as though the scenes were being specially rehearsed for our benefit.

Investigations into the past conducted by these methods show how a long process of gradual evolution, slow but never-ceasing. They show the development of man under the action of two great laws – first the law of evolution, which steadily presses him onward and upward, and secondly – the law of divine justice, or cause and effect, which brings him inevitably the result of his every action, and thus gradually teaches him to live intelligently in harmony with the first law.

This long process of evolution has been carried out not only on this earth, but on other globes connected with it; but the subject is much to vast to be fully treated in an elementary book such as this. It forms the principal theme of Madame Blavatsky's monumental work, *The Secret Doctrine*; but before commencing that students are advised to read the chapters on this subject in Mrs. Besant's *Ancient Wisdom* and Mr. Sinnett's *Growth of the Soul*.

The book just mentioned will afford the fullest available information not only as to man's past, but as to his future; and thought he glory that awaits him is such as no tongue can tell, something at least may be understood of the earlier stages which lead to it. That man is divine even now, and that he will presently unfold within himself the potentialities of divinity, is an idea which appears to shock some good people, and to be considered by them to savor of blasphemy. Why it should not be so is not easy to see, for Jesus himself reminds the Jews around Him of the saying in their Scriptures, "I said, ye are Gods," and the doctrine of the deification of man was quite commonly held by the Fathers of the Church. But in these later days much of the earlier and purer doctrine has been forgotten and misunderstood; and the truth now seems to be held in its fullness only by the student of occultism.

Sometimes men ask why, if man was at the first a spark of the Divine, it should be necessary for him to go through all these æons of evolution, involving so much sorrow and suffering, only in order to be still Divine at the end of it all. But those who make this objection have not yet comprehended the scheme. That which came forth from the Divine was not yet man – not yet even a spark, for there was no developed individualization in it. It was simply a great cloud of Divine essence, though capable of condensing eventually into many sparks.

The difference between its condition when issuing forth and when returning is exactly like that between a great mass of shining nebulous matter, and the solar system which is eventually formed out of it. Its condition when issuing forth and when returning is exactly like that between a great mass of shining nebulous matter, and the solar system which is eventually formed out it. The nebula is beautiful, no doubt, but vague and useless; the suns formed from it by slow evolution pour life and heat and light upon many worlds and their inhabitants.

Or we may take another analogy. The human body is composed of countless millions of tiny particles, and some of them are constantly being thrown off from it. Suppose that it were possible for each of these particles to go through some kind of evolution by means of which it would in time become a human being, we should not say that because it had been in a certain sense human at the beginning of that evolution it had, therefore , not gained anything when it reached its end. The essence comes forth as a mere outpouring of force, even though it be Divine force; it returns in the form of thousands of millions of mighty adepts, each capable of himself developing into a Logos.

Thus it will be seen that we are abundantly justified in the statement that the future of man is a future to whose glory and splendor there is no limit. And a most important point to remember is that this magnificent future is for all without exception. He whom we call the good man – that is, the man whose will moves with the Divine Will, whose actions are such as to help the march of evolution – makes rapid progress on the upward path; while the man who unintelligently opposes himself to the great current by striving to pursue selfish aims instead of working for the good of the whole, will be able to progress only very slowly and erratically.

But the Divine Will is infinitely stronger than any human will, and the working of the great scheme is perfect. The man who does not learn his lesson first time has simply to try over and over and over until he does learn it; the Divine patience is infinite, and sooner or later every human being attains the goal appointed for him. There is no fear and no uncertainty, but only perfect peace for those who know the Law and the Will.

PART XV:
CAUSE AND EFFECT

In previous chapters we have constantly had to take into consideration this mighty law of action and reaction under which every man necessarily receives his just deserts; for without this law the rest of the Divine scheme would be incomprehensible to us. It is well worth our while to try to obtain a true appreciation of this law, and the first step towards doing that is to disabuse our minds entirely of the ecclesiastical idea of reward and punishment as following upon human action.

It is inevitable that we should connect with that idea the thought of a judge administering such reward or punishment, and then at once follows the further possibility that the judge may be more lenient in one case than in another, that he may be swayed by circumstances, that an appeal may be made to him, and that in that way the incidence of the law may be modified or even escaped altogether. Every one of these suggestions is in the highest degree misleading, and the whole body of thought to which they belong must be exorcised and utterly cast out before we can arrive at any real understanding of facts.

If a man put his hand on a bar of red-hot iron, under ordinary circumstances he would be badly burnt; yet it would not occur to him to say that God had punished him for putting his hand on the bar. He would realize that what had happened was precisely what might have been expected under the action of the laws of Nature, and that one who understood what heat is and how it acts could explain exactly the production of the burn.

It is to be observed that the man's intention in no way affects the physical result; whether he seized that bar in order to do some harm with it or in order to save someone else from injury, he would be burnt just the same. Of course, in other and higher ways the results would be quite different; in the one case he would have done a noble deed, and would have the approval of his conscience, while in the other he could feel only remorse. But the physical burn would be there in one case just as much as in the other.

To obtain a true conception of the working of this law of cause and effect we must think of it as acting automatically in exactly the same way. If we have a heavy weight hanging from the ceiling by a rope, and I exert a certain amount of force in pushing against that weight, we know by the laws of mechanics that the weight will press back against my hand with exactly the same amount of force; and this reaction will operate without the slightest reference to my disturbing its equilibrium. Similarly the man who commits an evil action disturbs the equilibrium of the great current of evolution; and that mighty current invariably adjusts that equilibrium at his expense.

It must not be therefore supposed for a moment that the intention of the action makes no difference; on the contrary it is the most important factor connected with it, even though it does not affect the result upon the physical plane. We are apt to forget that the intention is itself a force, and a force acting upon the mental plane, where the matter is so much finer and vibrates so much more rapidly than on our lower level, that the same amount of energy will produce enormously greater effect.

The physical action will produce its result on the physical plane, but the mental energy of the intention will work out its own result simultaneously in the matter of the mental plane, totally irrespective of the other; and its effect is certain to be very much the more important of the two. In this way it will be seen that an absolutely perfect adjustment is always achieved; for however mixed the motives may be, and however good and evil may be mingled in the physical results, the equilibrium will always be perfectly readjusted, and along every line perfect justice must be done.

We must not forget, that it is the man himself and no other who builds his future character as well as produces his future circumstances. Speaking very generally, it may be said that, while his actions in one life produce his environment in the next, his thoughts in the one life are the chief factors in the evolution of his character in the next. The method by which all this works is an exceedingly interesting study, but it would take far too long to detail it here; it may be found very fully elaborated in Mrs. Besant's manual on *Karma*, and also in the chapter referring to this subject in her *Ancient Wisdom*, and in Mr. Sinnett's *Esoteric Buddhism*, to which the reader may be referred.

It is obvious that all these facts furnish us with exceedingly good reason for many of our ethical precepts. If thought be a mighty power capable of producing upon its own plane results far more important than any that can be achieved in physical life, then the necessity that man should control that force immediately becomes apparent. Not only is the man building his own future character by means of his thought, but he is also constantly and inevitably affecting those around him by its means.

Hence there lies upon him a very serious responsibility as to the use which he makes of this power. If the feeling of annoyance or hatred arises in the heart of the ordinary man, his natural impulse is to express it in some way either in word or in action. The ordinary rules of civilized society, however, forbid him to do that, and dictate that he should as far as possible repress all outward sign of his feelings.

If he succeeds in doing this he is apt to congratulate himself, and to consider that he has done the whole of his duty. The occult student, however, knows that it is necessary for him to carry his self-control a great deal further than that, and that he must absolutely repress the thought of irritation as well as its outward expression. For he knows that his feelings set in motion tremendous forces upon the astral plane, that these will act against the object of his irritation just as surely as a blow struck upon the physical plane, and that in many cases the results produced will be far more serious and lasting.

It is true in a very real sense that thoughts are things. To clairvoyant sight thoughts take definite form and color, the latter, of course depending upon the rate of vibration connected with them. The study of these forms and colors is of great interest. A description of them illustrated with colored drawings will be found in the book entitled *Thought Forms*.

These considerations open up to us possibilities in various directions. Since it is easily possible to do harm by thought, it is also possible to do good by it. Currents may be set in motion which will carry mental help and comfort to many a suffering friend, and in this way a whole new world of usefulness opens before us. Many a grateful soul has been oppressed by a feeling that for want of physical wealth he was unable to do anything in return for the kindness lavished upon him by another; but here is the method by which he can be of the greatest service to him in a realm where physical wealth or its absence makes no difference.

All who can think can help others: and all who can help others ought to help. In this case, as in every other, knowledge is power, and those who understand the law can use the law. Knowing what effects upon themselves and upon others will be produced by certain thoughts, they can deliberately arrange to produce these results. In this way a man can not only steadily mold his character in his present life, but can decide exactly what it shall be in the next.

For a thought is a vibration in the matter of the mental body, and the same thought persistently repeated evokes corresponding vibrations (an octave higher, as it were) in the matter of the causal body. In this way qualities are gradually built into the soul itself, and they will certainly reappear as part of the stock-in-trade with which he commences his next incarnation.

It is in this way, by working from below upwards, that the faculties and qualities of the soul are gradually evolved, and thus man takes his evolution largely into his own hands and begins to co-operate intelligently in the great scheme of the Deity. For further information on this subject the best book to study is Mrs. Besant's *Thought Power, its Control and Culture*.

PART XVI:
WHAT THEOSOPHY DOES FOR US

It must already be obvious to the careful reader how utterly these Theosophical conceptions change the man's entire view of life when he once becomes fully convinced of them ; and the direction of many of these changes, and the reasons on which they are based, will have been seen from what has already been written.

We gain from Theosophy a rational comprehension of that life which was before for so many of us a mere unsolved problem – a riddle without an answer. From it we know why we are here, what we are expected to do, and how we ought to set to work to do it. We see that, however little life may seem worth living for the sake of any pleasures or profits belonging exclusively to the physical plane, it is very emphatically worth living when regarded merely as a school to prepare us for the indescribable glories and the infinite possibilities of the higher planes.

In the light of the information which we acquire, we see not only how to evolve ourselves, but also how to help others to evolve – how by thought and action to make ourselves most useful, first of all to the small circle of those most closely associated with us or those whom we especially love, and then gradually by degrees, as our power increases, to the entire human race.

By feelings and thoughts such as these we find ourselves lifted altogether to a higher platform, and we see how narrow and despicable is the petty and personal thought which has so often occupied us in the past. We inevitably begin to regard everything not merely as it affects our infinitesimal selves, but from the wider standpoint of its influence upon humanity as a whole.

The various troubles and sorrows which come to us are so often seen out of all proportion because they are so near to us; they seem to obscure the whole horizon, as a plate held near the eyes will shut out the sun, so that we often forget that "the heart of being is celestial rest." But Theosophical teachings brings all these things into due perspective, and enables us to rise above these clouds, to look down and see things as they are, and not merely as they appear when looked at from below by very limited vision.

We learn to sink altogether the lower personality, with its mass of delusions and prejudices and its inability to see anything truly; we learn to rise to an impersonal and unselfish standpoint, where to do right for right's sake seems to us the only rule of life, and to help our fellowman the greatest of joys. For it is a life of joy that now opens before us. As the man evolves, his sympathy and compassion increase, so that he becomes more and more sensitive to the sin and sorrow and suffering of the world.

Yet at the same time he sees more and more clearly the cause of that suffering, and understands ever more and more fully that, in spite of it all, all things are working together for the final good of all. And so there comes to him not only the deep content and absolute security which is born of the certainty that all is well, but also the definite and radiant joy derived from the contemplation of the magnificent plan of the Logos, and of the steady and unfailing success with which that mighty scheme moves to its appointed end.

He learns that God means us to be happy, and that it is definitely our duty to be so, in order that we may spread around us vibrations of happiness upon others, since that is one of the methods by which we may lighten the sorrow of the world. In ordinary life a great part of the annoyance which men feel in connection with their various troubles is often caused by a feeling that they come to them unjustly. A man will say: "Why should all this come to me? There is my neighbor, who is in no way a better man than I, yet he does not suffer from sickness, from loss of friends, or loss of wealth? Why then should I?"

Theosophy saves its students from this mistake, since it makes it absolutely clear to them that no undeserved suffering can ever come to any man. Whatever trouble we may encounter is simply of the nature of a debt that we have incurred; since it has to be paid, the sooner it is cleared off the better. Nor is this all; for every trouble is an opportunity for development. If we bear it patiently and bravely, not allowing it to crush us, but meeting it and making the best of it, we thereby evolve within ourselves the valuable qualities of courage, perseverance, determination; and so out of the result of our sins of long ago we bring good instead of evil.

As has before been stated, all fear of death is entirely removed for the Theosophical student, because he understands fully what death is. He no longer mourns for those who have gone before, because they are still present with him, and he knows that to give way to selfish grief would be to cause sadness and depression to them. Since they are very near to him, and since the sympathy between them and himself is closer than ever before, he is well aware that uncontrolled grief in him will assuredly reflect itself upon them.

Not that Theosophy counsels him to forget the dead; on the contrary, it encourages him to remember them as often as possible, but never with selfish sorrow, never with a longing to bring them back to earth, never with thought of his apparent loss, but only of their great gain. It assures him that a strong loving thought will be a potent factor in their evolution, and that if he will but think rightly and reasonably about them he may render them the greatest assistance in their upward progress.

A careful study of the life of man in the period between his incarnations shows how small a proportion this physical life bears to the whole. In the case of the average educated and cultured man of any of the higher races, the period of one life – that is to say of one day in the real life – would average about fifteen hundred years. Of this period perhaps seventy or eighty years would be spent in physical life, some fifteen or twenty upon the astral plane, and all the rest in the heaven-world, which is therefore by very far the most important part of man's existence.

Naturally these proportions vary considerably for different types of men, and when we come to consider the younger souls, born either in inferior races or in the lower ranks of our own, we find that these proportions are entirely changed, for the astral life is likely to be much longer and the heaven-life much shorter. In the case of the absolute savage there is scarcely any heaven-life at all, because he has not yet developed within himself the qualities which alone enable the man to attain that life.

The knowledge of all these facts gives a clearness and certainty to our anticipations of the future which is a welcome relief from the vagueness and indecision of ordinary thought on these subjects. It would be impossible for a Theosophist to have any fears about his "salvation," for he knows that there is nothing for man to be saved from except his own ignorance, and he would consider it the grossest blasphemy to doubt that the will of the Logos will assuredly be fulfilled in the case of every one of his children.

No vague "eternal hope" is his, but utter certainty, born of his knowledge of the eternal law. He cannot fear the future, because he knows the future; so his only anxiety is to make himself worthy to bear his part in the mighty work of evolution. It may well be that there is very little that he can do as yet; yet there is none but can do something, just where he stands, in the circle around him, however lowly it may be.

Every man has his opportunities, for every connection is an opportunity. Everyone with whom we are brought into contact is a soul who may be helped – whether it be a child born into the family, a friend who comes into our circle, a servant who joins our household – everyone gives in some way or other an opportunity. It is not for a moment suggested that we should make ourselves nuisances by thrusting our opinions and ideas upon every one with whom we come in contact, as the more ignorant and tactless of our religious friends sometimes do; but we should be in an attitude of continual readiness to help.

Indeed, we should ever be eagerly watching for an opportunity to help, either with material aid, so far as that may be within our power, or with the benefit of our advice or our knowledge, whenever those may be asked for. Often cases arise in which help by word or deed is impossible for us; but there can never be a case in which friendly and helpful thought cannot be poured forth, and none who understands the power of thought will doubt as to its result, even though it may not be immediately visible upon the physical plane.

The student of Theosophy should be distinguishable from the rest of the world by his perennial cheerfulness, his undaunted courage under difficulties, and his ready sympathy and helpfulness. Assuredly, in spite of his cheerfulness he will be one who takes life seriously – one who realizes that there is much for each to do in the world, and no time to waste. He will see the necessity for gaining perfect control of himself and his various vehicles, because only in that way can he be thoroughly fitted to help others when the opportunity comes to him.

He will range himself ever on the side of the higher rather than the lower thought, the nobler rather than the baser; his toleration will be perfect, because he sees the good in all. He will deliberately take the optimistic rather than the pessimistic view of everything, the hopeful rather than the cynical, because he knows that to be always fundamentally the true view – the evil in everything being necessarily the impermanent part, since in the end only the good can endure.

Thus he will look ever for the good in everything, that he may endeavor to strengthen it; he will watch for the working of the great law of evolution, in order that he may range himself on its side, and contribute to its energy his tiny stream of force. In this way, by striving always to help, and never to hinder, he will become, in his small sphere of influence, one of the beneficent powers of Nature; in however lowly a manner, at however unthinkable a distance, he is yet a fellow worker together with God – and that is the highest honor and the greatest privilege that can ever fall to the lot of man.

www.ingramcontent.com/pod-product-compliance
Lightning Source LLC
LaVergne TN
LVHW041634070426
835507LV00008B/622